We have something
Magical.
Something that keeps us
Together.
No matter what,
In the deepest part
Of me,
There is part
Of you.

I'm afraid what holding

Onto you will mean.

But I'm afraid what letting

You go will do.

If only the people

In my life

Could learn to see you

Like I have come to.

Then,

I do not think

I would be so

Afraid.

You and I

Are made from

Stardust.

Let's keep it

That way.

We haven't said

Those three weighty

Words yet.

But,

I find myself

Thinking them

More and more.

What am I without you,

And you without me?

Nothing.

Like every drop of

Meaning would be squeezed

Out of life

If I were

Without you.

I can't remember

When we began…

The moment when

The line was crossed

Between friends

And something more than friends,

It seemed inevitable.

I wonder:

Are we *fated*

To be together

Or *destined*

To be together?

All I know is,

I want us

To be together.

Sometimes I fear

That you mean more

To me

Than I do

To you.

But when you

Look at me,

I see

The truth.

The possibilities

Of us together

Seem endless

And learning

About you

Seems even

vaster.

It was a year

A year ago today

When I told you

Goodbye

For what we thought

Was forever.

It felt like

Death

To go on living

Without you.

Months went by

And I thought I had

Moved on.

But,

when I saw

You were still there

Waiting...

Before I knew it,

You and I

Were back.

When I wake up,

My first thought is you.

Any thought

Before coffee

In the morning is

A big deal.

A day without

You

Is a

Dark day

Of the soul.

I had loved

Before you

But now that

Seems a lifetime

Away.

I know

That you loved

Before me.

But with us,

That no longer

Matters.

You are crazier than me.

I am the cautious one.

You pull me

Out of my comfort zone,

Beyond the familiar

Of everyday life.

With your encouragement,

And sometimes a push,

Dreams become

Reality.

I know

You would

Do anything

For me.

Even the

Slightest need,

You are always

Looking

To see if

I need something

Fixed or improved.

A defender

Or to break away

And have some

Fun.

I love seeing

Those moments

When you

Are proud of

Something you have

Worked hard

To accomplish.

There are two sides

To you:

The hard serious

Hard working side-

And the weird

Crazy fun side.

I want to say

Thank you for

Giving me the

Privilege to

See both.

It feels like

A day

Has never

Truly begun

Or ended

Until

I hear from

You.

I really do appreciate

Who you are.

I've never felt so free

To be myself

Than when I'm around you.

Expectations

Don't govern my reality.

You push me to become

A better me

And yet you somehow

Also accept me for who

I am today.

I feel like

I am enough

With you

And you will

Forever be enough

For me.

Will you open

Up the gates

Of your

Fortress?

I promise I

Will not

Betray your

Trust.

I will try

My best

Never to

Take you for granted.

Your vulnerabilities,

Who you are,

Will be safe

With me.

When I close my eyes,

I see a beautiful

Painting of

My current view of

Perfection.

When I open my eyes,

I see possibilities

On how to get there

But open or closed,

I always see

You.

I appreciate how

You treat me.

I used to wonder

If I opened

Up to someone,

If they would take

Advantage of me.

But with you,

You study me.

everything you learn,

You treat it as gold

And sometimes

I'm shocked

By how well you

Know me.

I know

you would never

Take advantage

Of that.

What we have

is real.

That used to

Terrify me.

But now that

I know you,

the reality

Of us

Both terrifies and

Excites me.

With you,

I feel safe

Safe in knowing,

When I turn

To you,

you have my

Best interest

In mind.

There are still some

Things

We haven't discussed.

Like,

How it felt

To say

Goodbye

And all those months

Of winter

Without you

And how we really

Feel about

One another.

But we won't rush

Those conversations.

I know we both

Prefer to let

It all happen

Naturally.

Actions speak

Louder than

Words

I know you've

Been hurt before.

Sometimes, when

I look at you,

I can see

The scar

That marks

A once

Torn apart heart.

I understand

Your caution

To let me in.

What do I see

When I look at you?

Someone

I can grow with.

A fellow dreamer

And explorer.

Someone who thinks

Similar enough to me

That communicating

Is simple.

But different enough

That it's

Intriguing.

Most importantly,

I see you.

And you

Just being you

Is forever enough.

I remember when

You told me

That you felt

You had

Known me

For years

When we had

Only known

Each other

For months.

And even now

After some time

Has passed,

I feel like I

Have known you

My whole

Life.

You are

A missing part

Of me

That I have finally

Found.

It's funny…

When I'm with

You,

I can't stop

Smiling.

Even though

My face

Hurts.

Sometimes I have

Nothing to say.

Still,

I want to say it

To you.

And

Still,

You Listen.

We are both

Independent souls

With an independent

Longing for

One another.

So, let's be

Independent together.

Spending time with you

Is crazy.

We can talk about

The deep issues

Of life

And then act like

Complete imbeciles

in the next

Breath.

I feel comfortable

With you.

It's okay to be

Vulnerable.

You are

Vulnerable

With me.

It feels safe,

Comfortable

But most importantly,

It feels

Healthy.

I want to be

As much of

A support to

You

As you are to

Me.

I want to celebrate

Your successes

As much as

You

Celebrate mine.

I want to walk

Beside You

As you reach

Your dreams.

Did life really

Exist before

I met you?

Sometimes I

Wonder if

It really did.

Certainly not

To its full

Capacity.

Sometimes,

I question

Whether I'm

Doing the right

Thing.

Are you really

The right one

For me?

I can find

No fault

In you.

Rose colored

Glasses on or

Off

A new year has

Begun.

Last year

I thought I had

Left you in

The past.

This year,

I know I'm

Bringing you

With me

Into the

Future.

What an odd

Phenomenon.

What will this

New year

Bring us?

Let's find out.

You and me

Together,

One moment

At a time.

I love how

You send me things

Randomly

Throughout the day

Just to

Let me know

You're thinking

About me.

Some things between us

Are too sacred

To expose

With a pen

And I know I will

Never forget them,

For they are

Impressed on a heart

Not merely written

On a page.

Sometimes

I think about

What life

Would be

Without you.

You've opened

My mind

To new ways

Of seeing

The world.

I think

Some of my

Projects

Were inspired

By you.

One thing is for certain:

Without you,

I would have

Gotten more

Sleep.

We are so

Similar

You and I.

So afraid to

Fall

Yet so ready

To take the

Leap.

You

Are so sure

Of your

Opinions

But

So afraid

Of your

Emotions.

I want you

To know,

I accept you

That way.

What a weird

Creature

Love is.

In its early

Stages,

Too afraid

To let you

Go.

Yet, just as

Afraid to

Let you

In.

Am I making

The right

Decision

Investing so much

Of me

Into you?

Is it normal

To feel what

I feel

For you

And yet question

What we

Are?

I know

You won't

Take advantage

Of me.

I know

That you truly

Care.

Maybe I am not

Doubting you…

Maybe

I am doubting

Me.

I'm so

Afraid

To ask

What we

Are

Because

I'm not

Sure

If we are

Ready

To really

Become

An us.

Why

Can I not

Make up

My mind

If I want you?

Yes.

Do I want us?

Yes.

But do I really

Want you?

I'm not sure.

Do I really

Want us?

It's complicated.

There are a

Million ways

I could

Tell you

How I feel,

Ways I could

Show you.

But today

Is not the

Day.

You said

That you

Were glad

To not be the

Only one.

That there was

Someone

Out there who

Felt as different

As you.

And I'm glad

That someone

Is me.

Why is it

That I

Can feel

So close

To you

Yet so far

Away?

When I was

Just a girl,

I thought

Love would

Be something

Consistent.

That the feelings of

Love

Would always stay

The same.

It took me

A little while

In life

To realize

That things never

Stay the same.

And,

That's Okay.

You are

A private

Person.

I learned patience

In knowing

That you

Would

Open up

To me

In your time.

And I was

unafraid

Of the

Silence.

I look at

You

At how you

Look at

Me.

When I

Think about

How you value me,

I know how

Lucky I am

To have found

Someone like

You.

I have you

And in having

You,

It feels like

I have

Everything.

Tell me

Everything

About you.

The exciting.

The mundane.

What you

Dream.

What keeps you

Up at night.

Your greatest

Fears

And the things

No one

Knows.

I want to know

Everything.

Last night,

I had a

Dream

About us.

About what we could

Become.

I wonder if

We'll make that

Dream

A reality.

When did

It become

Natural to say,

Us

Instead of

You being you

And

Me being me?

Instead,

you and I created

This new creature called,

We.

I know we

Both really like

Us

But I also don't want

Us to lose

You and Me

In the

We.

When I see you,

I see someone

I know

I can trust

But who doesn't

Push me

Into trusting.

Someone who respects

My space

Yet asks for

My company.

Someone who

I know

Will be there for me

If

Or when

I need them.

Thank you

For being

You

Because you

Are pretty

Darn

Amazing.

Looking into

Your eyes

Must

Be the

Strongest

Chemical known

To man

Because

You have me

Hooked.

How is it

That every song

And everything,

Everywhere,

Has to do

With you?

But that's

Alright.

I don't

Mind being

Reminded

Of you

All the time

Getting to know

You

Has been a

Journey.

I've learned

A lot about

You.

About how you work,

And your view of life.

I've learned

A lot about

Me.

About my own

Strengths and weaknesses

And I've come to

Value you

And us more

The more

I learn.

I never want

To stop

Studying you.

You are my

Major

And I want

A PhD.

I don't think

Words

On a page

Or the

Blood

Of a pen

Could ever describe

What

You are

To me.

Someday,

If this life

Permits,

I'm going to

Show you

Everything

I've written

About you.

It wasn't just

Written

About you

It was written

For you

And because

Of you

What an amazing

Thing it is

That two

People

Such as us

Met.

Not just

That we met-

We were

Able to become

Friends.

Even more amazing

That our friendship

Grew into something

More.

Sometimes I wonder

If it were

Just chance-

It feels more

Like fate.

How wonderful

It is

To find someone

Who understands

You

And loves you

Despite

Your flaws.

It is rare

To find someone

Like you.

I've never met

Anyone

So similar to me

Yet so different.

It's like we are made

From the same

Material

Yet printed with

Different patterns.

I can talk

To you

About anything

Knowing that

You will

Tell me the truth

Even when

I don't want

To hear

It.

We've come so far

You and I

And I can't wait

To see where

Our journey

Takes us.

Sometimes

When I look

At you,

I see my

Future.

Other times,

I look at you

And I only see

Confusion.

I want

To tell you

That

I see you

For you.

We never seem

To run out

Of topics to

Discuss.

Everything with you

Feels natural.

Today,

Tomorrow,

A lifetime:

I want to

Spend it with

You.

I want you

To be my

Forever

While I am

Lost in the

Moment.

Every time you

Message me,

I smile at my phone

Like crazy.

I think it's become

Noticeable.

We have something

That is

Incredibly special.

Let's not waste it.

All the words

Inside of me

Seem to be

About you.

Without you,

My whole world crumbles.

My existence shakes.

Someone, please help.

I did not want it

To be this way.

I never intended to

Fall this hard.

You stole my breath

Away.

I never wanted

To end up on

Life support.

Do others love

Like this?

I fear I must

Be cursed.

I love too much.

No wonder it is

Called being lovesick.

Because I am

Sick of love.

I do not want to

Feel this throbbing,

This pain that

Somehow grew

Inside of me and

Burns whenever

We are apart.

I really

Care about you.

But sometimes,

I really

Don't understand

You

And it hurts.

Maybe

I get frustrated

With you

Because

I expect too much.

But I won't

Lower my standards

I know my

Value.

Day by day

I get to know

You more.

Sometimes, I don't

Like what I see.

But I know

Who you are

And I choose to

Value you.

The question plagues me.

Will we be able to last?

To conquer the

Storms of life

Alongside each other?

Or, will we fade?

Will the stresses of

Life steal what

We have?

This is my

Constant contemplation.

Do you feel

What I feel?

Or am I living

In a fantasy?

But then I also

Wonder why

I question everything.

You and I.

How is it that we

Think the same,

Yet our ideas

About life

Are so different?

I want to get

To know you

On a level

No one has before.

I want to

Be known by you

Like no one has

Known me before.

I love

That I can

Just be

Myself

Around you.

That you want

To know

The real me

Even though

It's not as

Pretty

As surface

Me.

When you are

Ready

To tell me

The deep things

Inside,

I will be

here to

Listen.

What is more

Amazing

Than finding

Someone

As amazing as

You?

The way you look

At me,

With your eyes filled

With sincerity

causes me to want

To share everything

I am with you,

To hold nothing back

Because

I trust you

And you trust me.

Sometimes the

Closeness we have,

Scares me.

I care about you

And the depth

That I care

Scares me.

How is it possible

To both love

And be afraid

Of loving?

I just don't want

To be hurt again.

Being in love

Is one of the

Most amazing

Feelings.

I want to make

It last

But I don't want

To make the wrong

Decision.

You've hinted

You want to take us

To the next

Level.

I don't want to

Disappoint you.

I want to be true to

Who I am

In loving you.

And I have already

Fallen for you.

Are we drifting

Apart?

I feel so

Distant from you.

You haven't changed.

You are still there for me,

As always.

It is I

Who has changed.

I have become distant

And I don't know

Why.

I care so much

For you.

Your victories

Have become mine

And I see that

Mine too

Have become yours.

I want to love

You

Like you deserve

To be loved.

You and I

Are meant to be.

You've hinted

You want to take us

To the next

Level

I don't want to

Disappoint you

I want to be true to

Who I am

But I have already

Fallen for you

Are we drifting apart?

Because I feel so

Distant from you

You haven't changed

You are still there ...

It is I

Who have changed

I have become distant

And I don't know

Why

Sometimes,

I'm not so sure

You see us . . .

Like I do.

And maybe . . .

Maybe

I am just being naïve.

Maybe I am living

In a fantasy.

Thinking that

You and I

Could become

Something more.

Why is it?

How is it . . .

That I can look

At you

One moment

And see someone

I know so well

And the next

I see nothing more

Than a stranger with

A familiar face?

I think

You are trying very hard

To show me

How much you

Truly care.

And I want you to know

How much that means

To me.

I wish others

Could see you

Like I see you.

Like, how all the words

In this book

Describe you.

Because even though

I am falling for you,

I am falling with

Eyes wide open.

Sometimes I wonder

If there is such a

Thing as soulmates.

Is there really only

One person out there

Who is perfect for another?

Or is it merely the

Compatibility of personalities

That effects the strength of relationships?

But really it doesn't matter-

I have you

And that is enough

For me.

We became something today.

It feels so natural.

Like life was always supposed

To be like this.

We really must be crazy

But everything feels like

It's meant to be this way.

So, I'm going with it.

Sunday, March fifteenth has

Become more than just

A passing moment.

We agreed to take

This slow.

It seems like the right

Thing to do.

Just to see where things

Would take us.

But then,

My emotions want to travel

At the speed of light.

I have to bridle them

And bring them back

To the truth of

Reality.

I have suspicions…

A lingering thought

That this

Is just the beginning

Of us.

www.ingramcontent.com/pod-product-compliance
Lightning Source LLC
Chambersburg PA
CBHW020258180726
47994CB00028B/2422